Not like Johnny

Not like Johnny

Evan Owen

Illustrated by Dan Pearce

Evans Brothers Limited

Published by Evans Brothers Ltd.
Montague House, Russell Square, London WC1B 5BX

First published 1974
Reprinted 1976, 1978

Printed and bound in Great Britain by
Hazell Watson & Viney Ltd., Aylesbury, Bucks
ISBN 0 237 29006 5 (limp)
ISBN 0 237 29040 5 (cased)   PRA 5784

1

The coffee bar was full. It was always busy on Saturday afternoons. The yard at the side of the coffee bar was full, too. It was full of motor-bikes.

Inside the bar the juke box was belting out a strong beat.

"That Jimi Hendrix! Wasn't he fantastic? I could play him all day, every day," said Liz.

She was at a table near the door. Kevin was with her. So was Mary, her best friend. Mary was tapping the Hendrix beat on the table with a coke bottle.

"Sure," said Kevin. "Hendrix was great." He drank the last of his coffee. "But this coffee isn't

great. It's muck!" He emptied the dregs into a glass ash tray.

"The little lad's playing boats! Look, Liz!" said Mary. She pointed to a floating match on the dirty brown liquid.

Kevin grinned. "Aw, get lost, both of you!" He unzipped the top pocket of his leather jacket.

"Here, take a look at this, Liz. And you, Mary," he said. He took a piece of paper out of his pocket. Then he spread it flat on the table, between a dirty spoon and a half-sucked Polo mint.

"See! What do you think of that? That, girls, is a *real* bike!"

The girls looked at the picture. A Honda CB750. Gleaming red and shining chrome. Top speed 120 mph.

"It's a nice colour," said Liz.

"Yes. It's a nice colour," said Mary.

"Women! What does the colour matter? It can do twenty over the ton!" said Kevin.

"Are you going racing, then? To the Isle of Man, like?" asked Liz.

"See yourself going round them hairy corners,

do you, Kev?" asked Mary. "With your name coming over the loudspeakers?"

"Course not," said Kevin. "It's not a racing bike, anyway."

"What's it cost?" asked Liz.

"Don't know," said Kevin. "Doesn't say."

"Give it here," said Liz. She looked at the small print. "It does, you know," she said. "£780."

"Well, I wasn't thinking of buying it," laughed Kevin. "Not this week, anyway!"

Two boys at the next table put on their helmets. "Coming, Kev?" asked one of them.

"Later," said Kevin.

They went out of the door of the coffee bar as Vic walked in. He was Kevin's friend. He wore a black leather jacket and black flying boots. You could see the white wool round the tops. He was carrying his helmet. That, too, was black, with a grinning white skull on the front.

Vic banged his helmet on the table and sat down.

"Sit down, why don't you!" said Liz, sarcastically. He was Kevin's friend but Liz did not like

8

him. She thought he was a big-head, a show-off.

Mary liked him, though. She went for him in a big way. "I think he's real dreamy," she told Liz when she first met him.

"How about a bit of fun, Kev," said Vic. "On the old main road. The boys are waiting. What about it, eh?"

"No, Kevin!" said Liz. She looked scared.

"No, don't go, Kevin. Please!" She knew what Vic meant by a bit of fun on the main road.

2

"Well?" said Vic, looking hard at Kevin. "Are you coming or aren't you? Can't wait all day."

Kevin looked at Liz. He knew what she was thinking, why she was scared.

Johnny. Johnny Case. She was scared he would get smashed up like Johnny.

*   *   *

One night, just before Christmas it happened. Kevin, Vic, and Johnny were belting up the main road. They were doing about 85, working up to the ton.

Vic was in front, Johnny behind, and Kevin last. Then Johnny opened his throttle wide and roared past Vic. He was grinning as he went by.

But they were too near Cottage Corner for that sort of speed. Johnny roared round that blind left-hander like a rocket, low over his handlebars. He must have thought he was doing the TT in the Isle of Man.

Parked lorry. No lights. Johnny saw it too late.

He swerved but not enough. The doc at the hospital said he was lucky to be alive. Both legs were smashed and his skull cracked. Six weeks later and he was still in hospital. They said he would never ride again.

*   *   *

That was what Liz saw when she looked at Kevin. Him in hospital like Johnny. But she didn't say anything more. She just looked at him.

"They'll be OK," whispered Mary. She thought Vic was great. He wasn't scared of anything. Nor was she.

"You coming, then?" he asked Kevin.

"I'll be OK, Liz," said Kevin. "Wait here for me if you don't want to come."

"Not likely, Kevin Tate!" she exclaimed. "If you want to end up like Johnny, that's your death. I'm going home."

Liz pushed her chair back and marched out of the coffee bar without a backward look.

"Right, Vic, Mary!" said Kevin. He took his helmet from under his chair and put it on. "What are we waiting for?"

3

They climbed on their bikes, kick-started the engines and revved up. They sounded good; full of power, straining to go.

Mary climbed up behind Vic, wrapping her arms round his waist. He wriggled a bit, settling himself in the saddle. Girls on the back could be a drag, he thought. But Mary, she's all right. She's no novice.

"As far as the roundabout and back in fourteen minutes," he said, grinning.

"You'll be lucky!" said Kevin. They had never done it under fifteen minutes.

"Always a first time!" shouted Vic. He roared away on to the road, Kevin on his tail.

This is great, thought Kevin, feeling the bike leaping and throbbing between his legs. Nothing can stop us now, nothing, nothing!

The two bikes roared round a cattle truck and past a private car, leaving them standing.

Mary pressed her face into Vic's back, feeling the

cold of the leather on her cheek. Her hair was streaming out from under her helmet, her eyes closed tight. She could feel the bike's vibrations coming through Vic's body. They seemed fused into one flying rocket. Vic, Mary, the bike. All one. . . .

* * *

"Not this time, then," said Vic when they got back to the coffee bar. He checked the stop-watch on his wrist. "Not bad, though, Kev! Look, 14.50. That's the best yet!"

4

Kevin called at Liz's house on his way home.

"Liz don't want to see you," said Spud. He was her young brother. His name was Arthur but they called him Spud. Kevin couldn't stand him. Little horror, he thought.

"Ask her again, Spud, will you," he said. "It's important." He wanted to show Liz he was all right. Johnny might get smashed up but not him.

"No use," said Spud, coming back. "She won't see you!" He stuck out his tongue and slammed the door in Kevin's face.

She wouldn't see him the next day, either. But on Monday evening she was in the coffee bar when he arrived.

Kevin frowned. She was with another boy. Tall, fair hair, blue eyes.

"So you're here," said Kevin. "Thought you were dead or something."

Liz took no notice of his bad temper. "This is Bert," she said. "Bert Styles. He's my cousin. Lives over the other side of town."

Bert nodded at Kevin, then looked at Liz. "Want another coffee, Liz?" he asked.

"I'll get 'em," said Kevin. "My round." After all, Liz was supposed to be his girl. But he wished she had come without her cousin. The blue-eyed git.

He collected the coffees and took them back to the table.

"Ta, Kev," said Liz.

"Thanks," said Bert. He took a sip from his cup. "Cheers."

"Cheers," said Kevin.

"What sort of bike you got, Kevin?" asked Bert. He was trying to be friendly.

"Bike? Oh, a BSA 350. A Gold Star. Why?" said Kevin. "What do you ride? A scooter?"

Bert flushed but before he could speak Mary said: "Shut up, Kev! Course Bert don't ride a scooter. You aren't the only one with a proper bike!"

Kevin had a temper. So had Bert. She didn't want them fighting.

"What you got, then?" asked Kevin. If the blue-eyed wonder had a bike he couldn't be all bad.

Bert looked at Liz and grinned. "As a matter of fact I have got a scooter," he said. Then as Kevin started to laugh he added: "I've got a proper bike, too. A Styles Special."

"A *what*?" shouted Kevin.

"A Styles Special," said Bert, smiling. "It's a Greeves 250 really. But I built it up myself. Put in an alloy head and an alloy tank. Changed the front forks. So it's a Styles Special!"

"Sounds like a competition job," said Kevin.

Now he *was* interested. A man who could build up his own bike was worth listening to. Even if he did have blue eyes.

"It is. I keep it for scrambles and trials," said Bert. "The scooter is good enough for going to work and riding round town."

"What's it like, in scrambles?" asked Kevin.

"You haven't done any racing, then?" said Bert.

"No. But I've watched it on the telly. Scrambles, trials, and the TT in the Isle of Man. That's what I'd like. Road racing. Round those corners flat out at 100!"

Bert shook his head. "Not for me. Boring, road racing, after cross country riding. On the road you've only got speed. When you're scrambling you're fighting everything—the ups and downs, the water jumps, the U turns, the weather. Now that's really exciting!"

They had forgotten all about Liz. "Don't mind me, you two cowboys," she said. "I'm only here for the coffee. Don't know why I bothered."

She took her coat off the back of the chair and went across the coffee bar to join Mary and Vic.

5

Kevin met Liz in the coffee bar the next day. They were early. Apart from two boys playing the fruit machine and the girl at the counter the place was empty. But Liz and Kevin were always early on Tuesdays. It was their night to go to the cinema.

"Where we going, Kev?" asked Liz. "That musical *Happy Days*, is on round the corner. It's a good film."

"But we've seen it twice already," said Kevin.

"Don't mind seeing it again," said Liz. "There's nothing else on worth seeing, is there?"

"Matter of fact, yes, there is. At the Odeon. *The Claws of the Monster*. My mate at work saw it last night. Said it's a smashing horror film. A real scream, he said."

"A real scream. Very funny. He's a proper comic, your mate, isn't he! I don't think!"

Kevin was crazy about horror films. He said they gave him bad dreams but he still liked them. He never missed one if he could help it.

Liz would rather have a musical. But she didn't mind horror films. They didn't frighten her. They only made her giggle.

"All right. This week we'll see *The Paws of the Monster*. But next week you'll go where I want."

"OK," said Kevin. "Only it's The Claws not The Paws. *The Claws of the Monster*."

"Claws, Paws, who cares?" said Liz. "Long as it's a real scream, like your mate said."

Just then, Mary came in with Vic. "You not gone yet?" she said. "You'll miss the trailers."

"Hang about a bit, Liz," said Kevin. "Want to ask Vic about next Sunday."

"What about next Sunday?" asked Vic.

"Well, me and Liz are going to Corton Park—on the bike. There's this big scramble. All the best riders will be there."

"Bert Styles has asked us," said Liz. "You know Bert, he's my cousin. He was here last night with us. Bert's one of the riders."

"Well, what about it? Are you coming with us?" asked Kevin.

"Maybe. I'll see," said Vic. "Make a change, I suppose. Not that I go much on scrambles myself. Too messy, all that mud and muck. How about you, Mary? Do you want to go?"

"Might as well," said Mary. She grinned. "We was thinking of going to Buck Palace for this garden party. But I don't expect Her Majesty will mind. Not just this once."

"Well, no need to make your minds up now," said Kevin. "Let us know tomorrow. Or Thursday. Come on, Liz! We shall be late!"

6

"Well?" said Kevin the next day. "Are you coming Sunday or aren't you? To the scramble?"

"Yes. We're coming. Mary wants to go. Don't know if it's the scramble she wants to see or that Bert Styles," said Vic, laughing.

They were sitting astride their bikes outside the coffee bar. Above the noise of the traffic on the main road they could just hear the sound of the juke box. Several other bikes were in the yard. They had been admiring a big and powerful German bike, a BMW.

"Noble of you, Vic! Going because Mary wants to. You going soft or something? That the only reason?"

Vic grinned. "Not really. I want to take a look at that bike of Bert Styles. The one you told me about."

"Oh, yes. The Styles Special he calls it. Bit of a big-head, calling a bike after himself."

"I don't know," said Vic. He patted the tank of his bike. "Dig this! This is Vic's Velocipede!"

"Should be worth taking a look at, anyway, Bert's bike," said Kevin. "Must be pretty good. Liz told me he's won several races on it. And if the weather's OK it will be an afternoon out."

"That will please my old lady," said Vic.

"Ever thought of riding in a scramble, Vic?" asked Kevin.

"Can't say I have," said Vic. "Can't say it's ever appealed to me. Sounds too much like hard work. Why? Have you?"

"Not till I heard Bert on about it. From what he

said it's worth having a go."

"You'd be no good at racing," jeered Vic. "You always chicken out on the main road when it comes to the crunch."

"I don't chicken out!" said Kevin. "I could beat you all ends up if I put my mind to it. Any time. But I don't go mad on the road like you. Or like Johnny."

He looked at his watch. "What time's Mary coming tonight?"

"She's not," said Vic. "She's doing her hair. Women are always doing their hair. I can never see any difference. But they keep doing it. Is Liz coming?"

"No," said Kevin. "Guess what! She's doing her hair too!"

"Well, then, what we hanging about for? How about a go up the main road before it gets dark? To see who's chicken!"

"OK, but not the main road," said Kevin. "Let's go on the Shenton road. Over them two bridges. Then I'll show you who's really chicken."

"What bridges? Oh, you mean them two hump-backs. Just before you get to that village—what's

it called?—Newton End."

"That's it," said Kevin. "Over the bridges I'll leave you standing like you was on a kid's bike!"

Vic pulled his goggles down over his eyes. Kevin tightened the strap on his helmet.

They kick-started their bikes and roared on to the road. With Vic in front and Kevin behind, they rode the three kilometres to the Shenton turn at a steady speed.

Kevin was thinking about what Vic had said. Chicken, am I, he thought. I'll show him!

He had kept his anger buttoned up. Nothing Vic liked more than to see he had made him angry. Kevin glared at Vic's back, a few yards in front, crouched over the handlebars. Just you wait, Mister Mighty Vic, he thought. Just you wait!

They turned left into the Shenton road and round another corner. Then Vic waved Kevin down. They stopped by a heap of grit at the side of the road.

In front of them the narrow country road was straight and empty.

"How far to the bridges?" asked Vic.

"About a kilometre," said Kevin. "There's an S-bend half way. Then a right-hander by Oak-tree Farm."

"All them cows and sheep," laughed Vic.

"Yes, that's right. Mind the farm entrance. It's blind. Just round the corner. Don't want to end up on a cow's back!"

"Then the bridges, eh?" said Vic.

"Just a little farther on," said Kevin.

"What's it going to be, then?" said Vic. "First over the second bridge is the winner? That OK?"

"Right!" said Kevin. "You nod when you're ready for off."

They revved up their engines. Vic nodded his head and they were off. Kevin let Vic take the lead. He knew the road better than Vic. Whenever I'm ready I can take him, he thought. And I know where that will be!

The road was dry. The road surface was good. There was no wind to bother them. A crowd of

birds rose squawking from an old tree as they shot away like shells from a gun. A farmer's dog dashed off the bank and through the hedge.

Vic had no eyes for birds and animals. Nor had Kevin. Behind their goggles, eyes were fixed on the road ahead. It was still empty. They were coming up fast to the first leg of the S-bend and Kevin prayed it would stay empty.

Both bikes were roaring along sweetly under the riders. The boys, flat on the tanks of their bikes, hardly moved. They seemed to be part of their machines.

But they were feeling every bump on the road. Vibrations shuddered through the frames, through the forks, up to the handlebars, into their arms.

Kevin knew it was a flat S-bend, safe enough if nothing went wrong. But Vic was not sure and slowed down so that Kevin found himself almost touching Vic's rear light. He slowed down himself, widening the gap.

They leaned their bikes through the first bend, then into the second, and out again on to the straight. Kevin grinned to himself. This was great!

There was a big sign on the bank. SLOW CATTLE CROSSING it said. Kevin and Liz had laughed at that when they first saw it. "If they're that slow they should give them some pills or something!" Kevin had said.

There was no time for jokes this trip, though. Both riders eased their machines back as they swung round the right-hander and past the farm entrance. In wet weather the road was greasy as a chip-pan, but not today.

Now they could see the first of the bridges, just past a clump of trees on the left of the road. Vic pressed his body even flatter on the tank.

"This is it!" he thought. "Up and over and he won't see me for dust!"

They hit the bridge almost together. Vic just about had his headlamp in front. Then it happened. What Kevin had been waiting for.

He knew that just over the top of the bridge was a bump in the road, made by a tree root. He knew but Vic did not.

They were going so fast, both bikes left the road. The bump was at the point where the wheels landed.

By keeping on the crown of the road Kevin

missed the bump. Vic hit it with his front wheel. He fought with his bucking handlebars and kept the bike on the road. But now Kevin was in front.

The second bridge was coming up fast. Suddenly the cab of a farm lorry loomed over the hump.

The boys saw it together. Vic slammed on his brakes and his bike screamed into a skid.

Kevin was too near the bridge to brake. If he skidded he would hit the parapet of the bridge. Or he would hit the lorry. In a tiny fraction of a second he wanted to brake. But he realized it would be suicidal and changed his mind.

Instead, he opened the throttle wide and shot through the narrowing gap between the bridge and the lorry. There were about fifteen centimetres to spare on each side. But he was through before he knew it.

As he pulled the bike up he thought, with a thrill of pride, how cool he had been. Then he realized he was shaking all over. But where was Vic?

He rode slowly back over the bridge. The lorry was just crossing the first bridge. There was no sign of Vic or his bike.

"Over here! I'm over here!" Then Kevin saw him. The bike was on its side in marshy ground off the road, its wheels spinning. And Vic was sitting by it, in five centimetres of water.

Kevin laughed so much he nearly fell off his bike. If Mary could have seen her wonderful Vic now! On his backside in a puddle.

"Go on! Laugh!" shouted Vic, pushing his goggles up on to his helmet. "When you've finished perhaps you'll help me out. If it's not too much trouble!"

Kevin pulled his bike on to its stand at the side of the road. Still laughing he picked his way across the marshy ground. "Now who's chicken?" he said. "But perhaps I should say who's a duck!"

"All right, all right," growled Vic. "You've had your joke. Now give me a hand with the bike."

7

On Thursday evening Kevin called for Liz. Twice he rang the bell. No answer. He rang again. Then an upstairs window opened and Liz leaned out.

"Oh, it's you," she said. "Early, aren't you?"

"Half seven, I said. Half seven it is," said Kevin. He looked at his watch. "Well, almost."

"Shan't be a minute," said Liz. "They're all out except me. I'm nearly ready." She closed the window. Kevin went back to his bike at the kerb and waited.

Liz came out soon. Under a raincoat that was hanging open she was wearing a new trouser suit, cherry red. Kevin whistled. "Like it?" asked Liz.

"Like what?" said Kevin, pretending he'd not noticed.

"This!" she said, opening her coat and kicking out a leg.

"Oh, *that*," said Kevin. "Yes, it's OK." Then, as Liz glared at him, he grinned. "All right, then.

Of course I like it. Great. Fantastic. Sure you
don't mind riding with me, Princess?"

They both laughed and Liz climbed up behind
him. She hugged him quickly as they moved away
from the kerb. "Remember my white slacks?" she
shouted. Kevin nodded and laughed.

*   *   *

It was the first time she had been out with him on
his bike. Last summer it was, the month after
they had left school. A very hot day in August.
Kevin had called to take her for a ride into the
country. She had never been on a pillion before,
and at first she was frightened.

Then she got the feel of it. She found she needed
to press close to Kevin, letting her body move with

his. He drove slowly for the first few kilometres. Then suddenly Liz wanted to go fast, fast, fast.

"What's the matter?" she shouted in Kevin's ear, "Something wrong? Won't it go faster?"

Kevin opened the throttle then and they roared along the road in the hot sunshine. Liz almost shouted out loud. It was wonderful! Her hair blown out behind her, the vibrations of the powerful machine. And her arms round Kevin.

When they pulled into a lay-by to have the sandwiches Liz had brought for them, her eyes were shining. "That was super!" she said as she climbed down. "Better than anything I've ever done! Smashing!"

But Kevin was looking down at her legs. He was not laughing. "Must have been that patch of wet tar," he said, "half a kilometre back, by the station."

Liz looked down at her white slacks, her beautiful new white slacks, and nearly died. They were covered with black spots.

*　　*　　*

But that was last summer, she thought. She had learned to be careful about what she wore on the bike. Perhaps she should have saved her new red suit for another time. But the roads were dry and

there was no wet tar. The coffee bar was only a kilometre away. They were just turning the last corner.

She smiled at her memories. Kevin was all right. She knew no other boy she liked better. Perhaps she really loved him but she was not sure.

They pulled up in the yard of the coffee bar. "Vic's here already," said Kevin. Liz jumped off the pillion. She gave Kevin a quick hug and kissed him.

"Hey! What's that for?" he asked. But Liz just grinned and ran ahead into the coffee bar.

8

Vic was all right after his spill. So was his bike. He was lucky. Had he skidded the other way he would have landed in a ditch. He might even have hit a tree.

"Look, Kev," he said, when they had pulled his bike back onto the road. "Don't tell the girls about this. I shouldn't have called you chicken. I didn't mean it. Honest."

"Oh, I don't know. Why shouldn't I tell them? Give them a good laugh. You sitting there in that stupid puddle!" said Kevin. He looked sideways at Vic and they both burst out laughing. "OK," he said. "I won't say a word. I suppose it was mean of me not to tell you about that bump. Just after the top of the first bridge."

"You mean you *knew*!" shouted Vic. "Well, I'll be. . . . All right, you rat. If you keep your trap shut about the puddle I'll say nothing about the bump."

Kevin had another reason for not wanting the story to get out. If Liz knew he had been racing on the open road, playing silly devils again, she would be mad with him. Real mad. And that I

can't take, he thought. Because she's right, dead right.

So when he joined Liz in the bar with Vic and Mary he only winked across the table at Vic. They both grinned.

"And what's that in aid of?" asked Mary.

"What's what in aid of?" said Vic.

"That silly grin of yours. What's the joke? Not that I expect it's worth hearing," said Mary.

"So you won't hear it," said Vic. "Do we have to tell you everything?"

"Hey! Stop that!" said Kevin. Any moment now, he thought, and Vic will give the game away. "We're here to enjoy ourselves, not to fight. Go and get the drinks, Vic. About time you stood a round!"

Mary was sitting back, chewing her knuckles. Kevin could see she was still mad with Vic. "How do you like Liz in her new gear, Mary?" he asked. Liz stood up and turned on her heels like a model.

"All right," said Mary. "I should know. I helped

her choose it. Anyway, it makes her look too good for you. Anything we wear makes us look too good for you two cowboys."

"Sorry, I'm sure!" said Vic, putting the drinks on the table. "If we'd known we'd have worn our dinner jackets, wouldn't we, Kev! And come in our top hats instead of crash helmets!"

"That I'd like to see!" said Liz. "You two on your bikes in top hats and dinner jackets!"

She looked up. "Why, hallo, Bert," she said. "Didn't see you come in."

"Look's like I'm just too late!" said Bert. "I shall have to get my own coffee. Keep a seat for me." He went over to the bar, stopping on the way to put a coin in the juke box.

"That the best you could find?" asked Kevin when Bert was back at the table.

"What do you mean?" asked Bert.

"That record. Elvis. Elvis the Pelvis. He's past it. Didn't you know?"

"That's what you think," said Bert. "For my

money he's still the greatest."

"Quite right, too!" said Mary. "He's still terrific."

"What I really came here for was to see if you're coming to the scramble," said Bert. "So I can look out for you."

"Yes, we're coming," said Vic. "All of us. You'd better be good!"

"How did you start?" asked Kevin. "Racing, I mean. In scrambles."

"I've been scrambling now for, let me think, about five years. On and off," said Bert.

"You mean sometimes you're on your bike, sometimes you're off?" said Vic, laughing.

"Shut up, Vic!" said Kevin. "You must have started when you were at school, then, Bert?"

"Yes, that's right. I was thirteen when I started."

"Cor! The boy wonder!" said Mary.

"I didn't know you could. Not while you went to school," said Kevin. "Where did you get the bread? For the bike, I mean?"

"My Uncle Fred," said Bert. "He's on Dad's side of the family, Liz. Have you met him ever?"

"Once," said Liz. "Last Christmas. He's got a garage, hasn't he?"

"Yes, he's got this garage, near where I live. And he's mad about scrambling, and trials, and grass track racing. Used to be real good, too. He's shown me his newspaper cuttings."

"Does he still race?" asked Vic.

"No, not for some time. He hurt his back in the

garage and had to pack up racing. But he told me all he knew about the game."

"And the bike? What sort of bike did you start on?" asked Kevin. "Are there special bikes for boys?"

"Well, there are, yes. Sort of mini-scramblers. But any light machine would have done. If I was riding in schoolboy events now, I could have a 125 Bultaco, or a 125 Husqvarna. They're just the job for junior racing. But Uncle Fred lent me his special lightweight BSA. He'd built it up himself."

"Give it a rest!" said Liz. "We're not all mad about bikes, are we, Mary. Bikes, bikes, all the time! Any more of it and I shan't come on Sunday!"

"I thought you said we were going on to the discotheque, Vic," said Mary.

"We are. Later," said Vic.

"Well, we are, anyway," said Liz. "You lot can stay here yapping about bikes all night if that's what you want. We'll find some other fellows to take us. Eh, Mary?"

"One more thing, Bert," said Kevin. "Just this, Liz, then we'll stop talking bikes. I promise. Are there any clubs, Bert, for boys?"

"Sure. I was in the town's Youth Motor Cycle Club. And there are special events for schoolboys. Like Junior Scrambles and Schoolboy Trials."

"Must be easy when you start at school," said Kevin. "I mean it must be easy to get into proper racing."

"Kevin!" said Liz, glaring at him.

"Better stop," said Bert, laughing. "Or we'll have a fight on our hands. Another drink, girls?"

"Ta, Bert," said Mary. "I'll have a coke."

"And I'll have another coffee," said Liz. "Then we shall have to go. Why don't you come with us? It's a rave, down at the disco, isn't it, Mary?"

"Sure! I'd like to. Thanks," said Bert. He went to the bar to get the drinks.

"But mind, Kev, and you, Vic," said Liz. "No more bike talk. OK?"

9

On Saturday night it rained. But by mid-day on Sunday the sun was shining. It was a good day to be out in the country.

Kevin called for Liz. This time she was ready and waiting for him. Corton Park was fifteen kilometres by road. The sun had dried the crown of the road, but there were puddles at the side. So Liz was wearing dark slacks and her old raincoat.

She had her crash helmet, too, this time. It was bright yellow, with a red band across the top. Kevin was always on at her to wear it, even when they only went to the coffee bar. He was right, of course.

"I know it makes a mess of your hair," he would say. "But better make a mess of your hair than make a mess of your head."

While she was settling herself on Kevin's pillion, Vic roared up on his bike, with Mary. She was wearing an old pair of jeans and a mock-leather coat. Her crash helmet was blue, with red spots all over it.

Vic had wanted her to get a helmet like his, with

a skull on the front. But Mary said it made her feel creepy. If he wanted to look like death that was his problem. One skull on the bike was enough.

She climbed off Vic's bike and went over to Liz. "Did you bring any food?" she asked. "I forgot to ask you if you wanted me to bring some sandwiches. So I've brought some, just in case."

"Just as well you did," said Liz. "I've only got enough for me and Kev. Didn't bring any drinks, though. Did you?"

"No need. Vic says there'll be places there for getting tea and coke."

"Come on, girl!" called Vic. "You going to stand there all day talking? Let's get moving. There's bound to be a lot on the road now the sun's out."

Mary made a face at Vic, but she ran over and climbed back on to the pillion. "All set, then?" shouted Kevin. Vic nodded. The boys pulled their goggles down over their eyes.

Liz waved to her brother, Spud, who was watching from the window. He had wanted to go with them. Kevin was glad there was only room for one passenger on a motor-bike!

The two bikes pulled away from the kerb. With Kevin and Liz in front, they drove down the street and on to the main road. Traffic was heavy. In both directions. Vic was right. The sunshine had brought motorists out in their thousands.

Big cars, small cars. Cars of all shapes and colours. Some with open tops, some pulling caravans, a few pulling boats. Old cars, new cars. Vans, three-wheelers, and a few lorries. All the vehicles in the country seemed to be on the road.

Now and again a motor-bike would shoot by in the opposite direction. But there were not many

bikes about. Not until they got nearer to Corton Park.

Both the boys were driving carefully. Speed was out of the question, and they were in no hurry. Kevin kept his bike well back from the vehicle in front. This was safer. It also kept him and Liz clear of the showers of muddy water thrown up when the car in front went through puddles.

He could not see Vic's bike in his mirror. They were separated by a big American car pulling a caravan. But he was not worried. Vic knew the way to Corton Park. In this sort of traffic it was not easy to keep together.

Liz was holding on tight. It was a bore, all this traffic. Not much to see anywhere. Only traffic and more traffic. But she kept very still. Kevin had enough to do, watching the car in front and the car behind, without having to bother about Liz.

After what seemed like an hour, they came to the turn to Corton Park. There was a blue sign pointing the way. Kevin swung his bike into the turning. He drove on for a few metres, then stopped. Then he saw Vic's black helmet with the white skull rounding the bend, and moved off again.

Suddenly the world seemed full of bikes, hundreds of them. All making for Corton Park. A few fools tried to be clever, cutting in and out of the stream of traffic. But they soon saw it was useless. The wide ribbon of bikes down the left side of the road moved noisily along towards the entrance to the Park.

10

Once inside, they parked their bikes. They had never seen so many in one place. Row on row of bikes, of all sizes and colours. From scooters to big powerful machines, some with sidecars. To Liz and Mary it was just a great heap of bikes. To the boys it was exciting.

"I've never seen so many different makes!" said Kevin. "Some of them I've never even heard of!"

"Must be hundreds and hundreds," said Vic. "But I'm not going to count them. Let's go and find Bert."

The track wound like a snake along the side of a deep hollow in the hills. All the way round it was lined with spectators. They were kept at a safe distance from the riders by a double fence of rope between stakes.

The start was marked by a big white banner across the track. After a straight stretch the track went out of sight among some trees. On the other side of the trees it dipped suddenly before shooting up and over a sharp ridge. Then came a long run down to a shallow stream at the bottom of the hollow. The riders had to ride through the stream

and climb again, up through a hairpin bend. Then a straight run to finish each lap under the banner.

The riders kept their bikes in a roped-off area near the start. Vic and the others were nearly there when a loudspeaker just over their heads made them jump.

"Next event, the Corton Trophy race, first heat. Looks like number 48 is having trouble getting started! What's wrong, 48? Forgotten how to start it? Ha! Ha! No, he's ready now. Over to you, Mister Starter."

"Hey!" shouted Kevin. He was looking at his

programme. "Bert should be in this one. It's down here. 'Number 37, B. Styles'. Can you see 37?"

"Yes, there he is!" said Liz. "Look! Second along this side. In a dark helmet."

"I like his riding gear, too," said Mary. "Dig that black and orange!"

Eight bikes with their riders were lined up under the banner, revving their engines. Then, with a deafening roar, they were off, front wheels rearing up as they opened their throttles.

The ground was wet and slippery after the night's rain. As the bunch of riders disappeared into the trees they sent a shower of mud over the nearest spectators.

"Bert's third!" shouted Vic, as the riders shot out from the trees. There was a gap between the first three and the rest of the bunch. Down they went into the dip, fighting to keep their machines upright, stabbing the ground with their feet.

Then they roared up and over the ridge, their bikes leaving the ground, both wheels clear by nearly a metre. The first three landed safely and roared away towards the stream. But the man who was lying fourth lost control when his wheels hit the ground.

His bike skidded round like a top, throwing him clear of the other riders. Somehow they managed to miss the fallen machine. Its rider got up slowly and stretched himself. He was all right.

"Now I know what that means!" said Mary. She pointed to a notice. WARNING TO THE PUBLIC . . . MOTOR RACING IS DANGEROUS.

"Do they have many accidents, Vic?" she asked.

"Depends on the state of the track," he said. "And how good the riders are. Usually a few spills. They're not often bad accidents."

WARNING
TO THE PUBLIC
MOTOR RACING
IS DANGEROUS

"There's a First Aid tent over there," said Liz.

"And an ambulance," said Kevin.

The riders had been through the stream with great splashes. Now they were sliding round the hairpin bend. Bert was still third as they finished the first lap.

"How many laps, Kev?" asked Liz.

"Three on this track, Bert says. Plenty of time for him to get up to first place."

There were no more falls. But one rider had to

leave the track when his engine failed. At the end of the second lap Bert was still third.

"Come on, Bert!" screamed Mary as he roared past.

As he came out of the trees for the last time he was level with the second rider. They rose into the air over the ridge together. Then Bert shot past into second place just before the stream.

"He could get first!" said Liz. "It doesn't look as if he's trying."

"No point," said Kevin. "The first two in each

heat go into the Final."

Sure enough, Bert finished second. They went into the roped-off area among all the racing bikes. Bert was down on one knee holding a spanner.

"Trouble, Bert?" asked Vic.

"Not really. But it wasn't going as well as it should. So I'm changing this plug. See? It's dirty. Did you see the race?"

"Yes. We saw it," said Kevin. "What chance have you in the Final?"

"A pretty good chance. The only chap who might beat me is in the heat that's running now. He beat me by a wheel in a race last Sunday. But I think I can take him this time," said Bert.

The boys bent over the machine with its studded tyres under the cut-off mudguards. They started asking Bert questions about the bike. The girls wandered off. They had seen an ice-cream van near the start. Maybe they could get a coke or something.

"Well, Kevin?" said Bert. "Fancy having a go? Now you've seen what it's like?"

"I don't know. Not yet," said Kevin. "I'll tell you after the meeting."

11

In the Final of the Corton Trophy race, Bert jumped into the lead from the start. Two other riders stayed with him for the first two laps. Then they dropped back. The rider Bert feared most was never in with a chance. He had trouble with his engine and did not finish the race. Bert was on his own. He won easily.

"Easy! Easy!" shouted Kevin.

"Too easy by half," grunted Vic. "I don't call this exciting."

"What do you want then, Vic?" asked Liz. "A lovely pile-up? Blood and bodies all over the place?"

"It's only Bert making it look easy," said Kevin. "You wouldn't find it that easy yourself!"

They had agreed to meet at the coffee bar that night. Bert was late. When he came in he went straight to their table.

"Have you made up your mind?" he asked Kevin. "I must know tonight. I'll tell you why in a minute."

"Yes. I think so," said Kevin, looking at Liz. But Liz was looking in her coffee cup. "Yes! I have. I want to have a go," he said.

They had been talking about it while they were waiting for Bert. Liz did not know what to say. If it would stop Kevin from going mad on the main road she was all for it. But it was still a dangerous way of having fun. She told Kevin he would have to make up his own mind.

"Good! That's what I wanted to hear!" said Bert. "Now listen. I've just been to see my uncle.

That's why I'm late. He's got a Greeves 250 he's been working on. He says it goes like a bomb."

"Sounds just the job," said Kevin. "But how much is it?"

"This is the best part of it. He says you can try it out first. If you like it he'll take your BSA off you and let you have a second-hand scooter to make up the value. How's that for a good swop? Your bike isn't worth more than about £180. You can't lose!"

"Scooter! Who wants a scooter?" said Vic.

"Kev does! To get to work," said Liz. "He can get a better bike later if he wants to."

"So you think it's a good idea, Liz?" said Kevin.

Liz smiled and nodded. It was the thought of the scooter that she really liked. With the scooter Kevin would never race on the main road.

"Right, Bert! It's a deal!" said Kevin. "When can I see the Greeves?"

"We'll meet at the garage tomorrow evening, then," said Bert. "I'll give you the address before I go."

"How do I start at scrambling? When can I have

my first race?" asked Kevin.

"Not so fast! All in good time. Get your bike first. Then we can see about the next step," said Bert.

"He's mad keen, our Kev, isn't he!" said Vic.

"You're not, then?" said Bert.

"Me? No. Too tame for me, scrambling. Road-racing, yes. Now that's what I call racing!"

When Bert had gone Mary turned to Liz. "Fancy you wanting Kev to go scrambling! Thought you were against him going racing?"

"I was," said Liz. "But he wants to. So he must. It's better than cutting up motorists on the road!"

"One good thing," said Mary. "There's always an ambulance at scrambles!"

"Sure!" said Vic. "And if he breaks his neck they can always send for a hearse!"

But Liz was not listening. She had been worried about Kevin racing on the road with Vic and the boys. Now she felt much happier.

As for Vic, he could please himself. He was Mary's problem.